THE FIFTH ANTI COLORING BOOK®

Susan Striker

An Owl Book
HENRY HOLT AND COMPANY   New York

In memory of Rose Mann

"What Kierkegaard said about love is also true of creativity: Every person must start at the beginning."

—Rollo May

Henry Holt and Company, LLC
Publishers since 1866
115 West 18th Street
New York, New York 10011

Henry Holt ® is a registered
trademark of Henry Holt and Company, LLC.

ISBN 0-8050-2376-3 (An Owl Book Book: pbk)

Henry Holt books are available for special promotions and premiums. For details contact: Director, Special Markets.

Printed in the United States of America

9   10   11   12   13   14   15   16   17   18   19   20

Illustrations by Joe Dyas, Judy Francis, Randi Katzman, Edward Kimmel, Maggie MacGowan, and Susan Striker

The Anti-Coloring Book is a registered trademark of Susan Striker.

Introduction

A good art activity serves many purposes for a child. It provides an opportunity for independent problem solving as the youngster works toward the completion of a goal. It gives pleasure through increased sensory awareness—in the smearing of finger paint, the molding of clay, or the blending of chalks. And it can be a magical way to help a child cope with fears and problems.

In her book *Child Art Therapy*, Judith Rubin says, "Giving form to the feared object brings symbolic control." Remembered nightmares, when drawn, take on form and thereby lose their sense of horror, permitting peaceful sleep. To a child the bogeyman and other monsters are not mere make-believe; they can be the personification of all the frightening things this world holds. Drawing, painting, and talking about such terrors are much more helpful for a child than being told that there is "no such thing as the bogeyman." Similarly, drawing feelings of aggression, anger, and hostility gives vent to the child's emotions, dissipating the rage.

Young children believe in the magic of art when it has real, personal meaning for them. I once taught an art lesson to first graders, in which the children were free to choose their own subject matter while working with limited colors. The room was completely quiet as the children concentrated on their work. I put a needle on a phonograph record, and when the music began playing, I heard one little boy say incredulously, "Oh, wow, I just started to paint a radio, and already there's music!"

Unfortunately, many school projects convince children that "art" means tracing and coloring. Time spent coloring in and tracing adult art is wasted time, but, more important, each "color in" experience further establishes the myth that art consists of the imitation of professionally drawn pictures and pushes children further away from open-ended opportunities of growing and learning about the world and themselves through self-expression.

Art therapist Margaret Naumberg says that all of her patients

…held in common the idea that art stems from an ability to trace or copy pictures. This misconception about art and the nature of the creative process is often derived from the kind of teaching still offered in many schools. While it obviously limits the growth of normal children, and constricts the development of their potentialities, it may do even more harm to children who enter school life without a sound personal orientation. For when art teaching is dealt with as a routine process, it discourages efforts at spontaneous and creative expression and forces pupils into a degree of stereotyped reproduction of known models that encourages regression and evasion of creative effort, even in normal children.

Art can provide the means for working through questions and dealing with problems. Even the most normal, well-adjusted child will encounter some difficulties while growing up—some serious ones, such as divorce, illness, or death in the family, and other simpler ones such as the birth of a sibling or a move to a new home. Art is one way for a child to assimilate and deal with his or her feelings. Parents and teachers who have learned to look closely at children's art know it adds immeasurably to communication as well.

For young children art is a language unto itself, and understanding this language is the key to helping children grow through art. Many adults fail to appreciate their children's artwork until realistic objects begin to be recognizable. They see a three-year-old's drawing as "just" a scribble, and instead lend encouragement to the child who draws a turkey by tracing around the fingers or pastes together a teacher-made pumpkin. But in fact several distinct stages have been identified in the development of children's art, encompassing both scribbles and recognizable shapes. To discourage progress through those stages is to stunt the child's development.

The first stage, lasting from ages one to four, is scribbling. Art educator Rhoda Kellogg has delineated a language of scribbling which consists of a vocabulary of approximately twenty shapes:*

·· ˆ	dot		roving enclosed line
│	single vertical line		zigzag or wavy line
—	single horizontal line		single loop line
\ /	single diagonal line		multiple loop line
⌒	single curved line		spiral line
ⱳⱳ	multiple vertical lines		multiple line overlaid circle
≣	multiple horizontal lines		multiple line circumference circle
⫻ ⫻	multiple diagonal lines		circular line, spread out
⟮	multiple curved lines		single crossed line
	roving open line	○	imperfect circle

*Illustrations adapted from *Analyzing Children's Art* by Rhoda Kellogg.

Until age three, children freely experiment with all or most of the basic scribbles, starting with random scribbling and becoming much more controlled and purposeful as they develop. At this stage children should be encouraged and praised for their efforts, for to dismiss a child's scribble as a "failed" drawing is like dismissing a child's tentative first step as "failed" walking. Both are acts parents can take pride in; both signify growth. It is important to note, however, that whereas children will walk with or without encouragement from adults, in order for a one-year-old to begin scribbling, he or she needs to be given appropriate materials and sensitive adult response. Parents and teachers who give encouragement to children through their scribbling stage are fostering healthy self-expression, self-reliance, and creativity. To misdirect children to draw realistically when they are not ready is to force them to skip essential steps in this developmental process. It is helpful for adults to express as much delight at seeing a spiral emerge on a page of scribbled dots and lines as they do when the child utters a first complete sentence.

At about age three, most children begin to add mandalas to their art. The mandala (Sanskrit for "circle") is a graphic symbol with three basic characteristics: it is symmetrical, it has a center, and it has cardinal points. To many cultures throughout the world, especially in the Orient and India, mandalas have great religious, spiritual, or mystical significance. Westerners rediscovered the mandala concept through the work of Carl Jung, who wrote that the mandala is "a basic structural device in the alchemical tradition of the West, and as a therapeutic, integrative art form created by patients in their own search for individualization." Children's mandalas usually take the form of crossed lines within a circle, oval, or rectangle. The lines both subdivide this shape and radiate from it.

With the mandala as a basis, children begin to draw realistic forms at about age four. The mandala becomes a sun, a wheel, or some other recognizable image. Very soon after, children start drawing human beings in shapes that spring directly from the mandala.

From about ages four to seven, children represent objects in their environment, choosing colors and sizes for emotional reasons rather than for accuracy. Parents should not try to force them to be more "realistic" in their choices.

Between approximately ages seven and nine, children develop a formula for drawing certain things they tend to use over and over. The concept of perspective is still a ways off and objects are depicted on a base line.

From ages nine to twelve, children become much more interested in and adept at creating things as they see them. They also become very self-conscious about their art and usually don't want to talk about their drawings.

There are several ways parents and teachers can help encourage creative growth in children. One is through sound choice of materials. Children should be permitted to choose from a variety of safe drawing, painting, and constructing materials, and to know that they will be given the opportunity to use them without restriction. If tidy housekeeping is of paramount importance, let a child use crayons that wipe off in water, or give a child "fingerpaints" made of food coloring and Ivory Snow to use on the lawn, in the wading pool, or in the bathtub. (But I believe a neat house is not an important enough excuse for depriving a child of unrestricted art exploration.) Finally, and most importantly, children respond to adult interest. It is through parents' demonstration of interest that children's artistic expression is most keenly stimulated.

© Susan Striker

© Susan Striker

Where will you go on your magic carpet?

© Susan Striker

What does the bogeyman look like?

Design a TV test pattern.

© Susan Striker

What does your dream car look like?

© Susan Striker

What do you like to do most at recess?

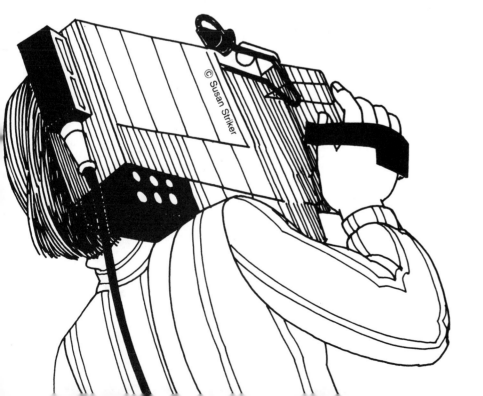

© Susan Striker

You're on assignment in a foreign country for ACB News. What story are you covering?

What treasure have you found in this **junk yard?**

© Susan Striker

Almost every great city has a tall building with an
observation tower on top. What city would you like to see from above?

You are an explorer in an undiscovered land. You have just seen prehistoric monsters still roaming the earth.

Entertain your parents with a tall tale!

© Susan Striker

You are the most famous and daring skywriter
in the world.

Daily

Volume MXXII November 3, 2983

World Events

Local News

The Arts

Sports

What will a newspaper look like in a thousand years?

How can you make your friends laugh?

The Fifth Anti-Coloring Book® / Owl Books

What would happen if you spilled salt and forgot to throw some over your left shoulder?

The Fifth Anti-Coloring Book® / Owl Books

© Susan Striker

Make your own sundae!

The Fifth Anti-Coloring Book® / Owl Books

What's going on down there?

© Susan Strik.

Are you ever tempted to tell a secret?

If you could fly your own airplane, where would you go?

What is your favorite thing about school?

© Susan Striker

Design a toy to play with in the bathtub.

© Susan Striker

What is the best story your grandparents tell about the old days?

If you and your friends dug a hole in your back yard as
deep as you could, where would you end up?

The Fifth Anti-Coloring Book® / Owl Books

You are a modern artist painting your interpretation of an outdoor scene.

Do you ever daydream when you should be working?
What do you daydream about?

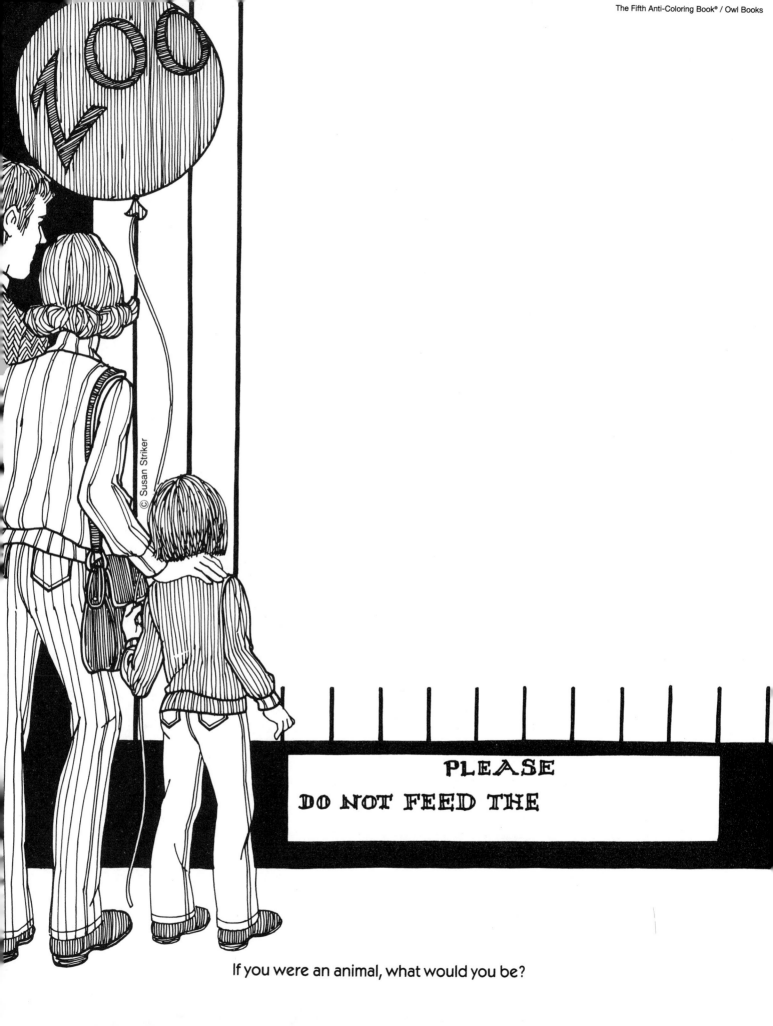

© Susan Striker

PLEASE

DO NOT FEED THE

If you were an animal, what would you be?

Did you ever spill milk and see pictures in it?

Why do these children want to get to the other side of the fence?

© Susan Striker

The Fifth Anti-Coloring Book® / Owl Books

This page is for the whole family to work on together!

You are the ringmaster of the circus. What act do you plan for the center ring?

© Susan Striker

How would you dress this doll?

The Fifth Anti-Coloring Book® / Owl Books

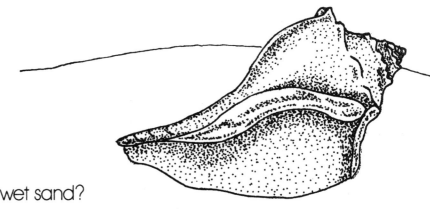

Do you ever make drawings in the wet sand?

© Susan Striker

If you ran away from home, where would you go?

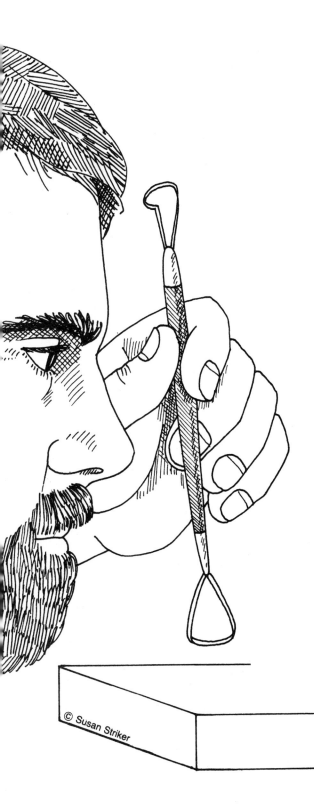

© Susan Striker

What is the sculptor working on?

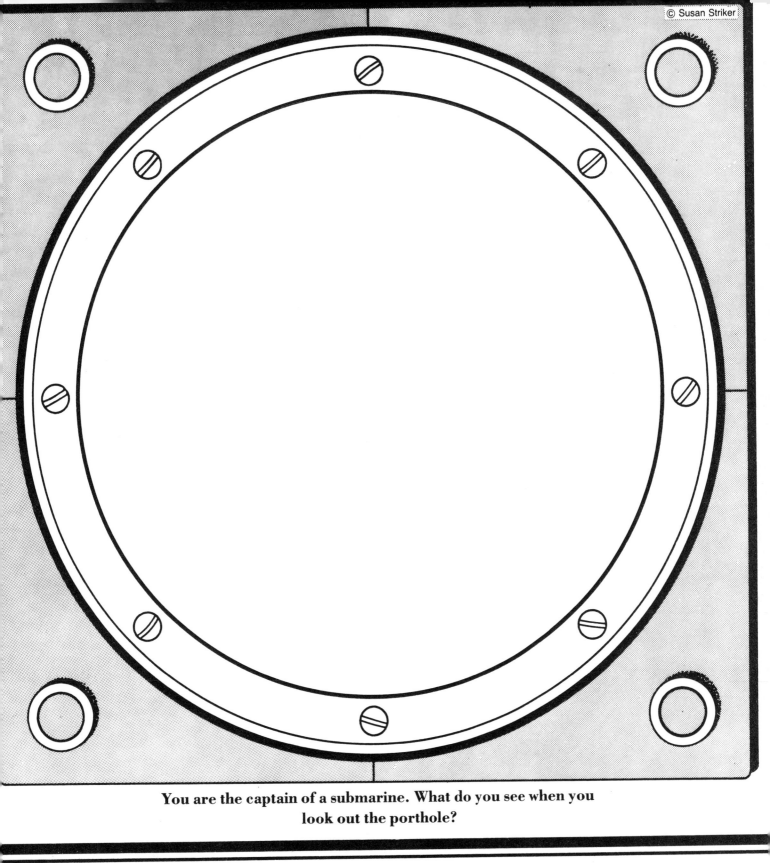

© Susan Striker

You are the captain of a submarine. What do you see when you
look out the porthole?

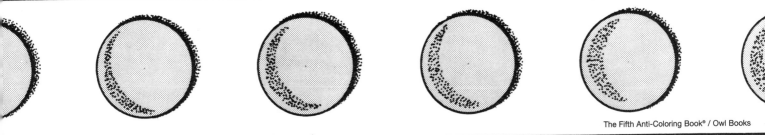

Add your family's portrait to this album.

The Fifth Anti-Coloring Book® / Owl Books

© Susan Striker

HOW WOULD YOU LOOK AS A CLOWN?

FIRST RUN

The billboard you designed is attracting
a lot of attention.

What would people look like without bones?

The Fifth Anti-Coloring Book® / Owl Books

Where would you go if you were a moonbeam?

© Susan Striker

**You are in charge of the school play this year.
What story will you produce, and who will star in it?**

© Susan Striker

PUT ON A SIDEWALK ART SHOW
WITH YOUR FRIENDS.

If you could cast magic spells, what would your first one be?

©Susan Striker

Design a mobile for the baby.

Where do you go after you die?

The Fifth Anti-Coloring Book® / Owl Books

The Anti-Coloring Book® by Susan Striker and Edward Kimmel
General interest, for ages 6 and older.
ISBN 0-8050-0246-4

The Second Anti-Coloring Book® by Susan Striker with Edward Kimmel
General interest, for ages 6 and older.
ISBN 0-8050-0771-7

The Third Anti-Coloring Book® by Susan Striker
General interest, for ages 6 and older.
ISBN 0-8050-1447-0

The Fourth Anti-Coloring Book® by Susan Striker
General interest, for ages 6 and older.
ISBN 0-8050-2000-4

The Fifth Anti-Coloring Book® by Susan Striker
General interest, for ages 6 and older.
ISBN 0-8050-2376-3

The Sixth Anti-Coloring Book® by Susan Striker
General interest, for ages 6 and older.
ISBN 0-8050-0873-X

The Anti-Coloring Book® of Exploring Space on Earth by Susan Striker
Architecture and interior design.
ISBN 0-8050-1446-2

The Anti-Coloring Book® of Masterpieces by Susan Striker
The world's great art, including color reproductions.
ISBN 0-8050-2644-4

The Inventor's Anti-Coloring Book® by Susan Striker
Inventions, devices, and contraptions.
ISBN 0-8050-2615-0

The Mystery Anti-Coloring Book® by Susan Striker
Mysteries, discoveries, and cops and robbers.
ISBN 0-8050-1600-7

The Newspaper Anti-Coloring Book® by Susan Striker
Write and illustrate your own newspaper.
ISBN 0-8050-1599-X

The Circus Anti-Coloring Book® by Susan Striker with Jason Striker
Clowns, acrobats, and everything else under the big top.
ISBN 0-8050-3412-9

The Anti-Coloring Book® of Celebrations by Susan Striker
Literature-based activities for holidays from around the world.
ISBN 0-8050-3414-5

Artists at Work by Susan Striker
A literature-based Anti-Coloring Book® on careers in art.
ISBN 0-8050-3413-7

Look for these at your local bookstore.